Successful
Recruitment
in a week

JOHN MACDONALD
JENNY RILEY

Hodder & Stoughton

A MEMBER OF THE HODDER HEADLINE GROUP

Orders: please contact Bookpoint Ltd, 39 Milton Park, Abingdon, Oxon OX14 4TD. Telephone: (44) 01235 400414, Fax: (44) 01235 400454. Lines are open from 9.00 - 6.00, Monday to Saturday, with a 24 hour message answering service. Email address: orders@bookpoint.co.uk

British Library Cataloguing in Publication Data
A catalogue record for this title is available from The British Library

ISBN 0 340 73816 2

First published 1999
Impression number   10 9 8 7 6 5 4 3 2 1
Year   2004   2003   2002   2001   2000   1999

Typeset by Multiplex Techniques Ltd, St Mary Cray, Kent.
Printed in Great Britain for Hodder & Stoughton Educational, a division of Hodder Headline Plc, 338 Euston Road, London NW1 3BH by Cox & Wyman Ltd, Reading, Berkshire.

the Institute
of Management

F O U N D A T I O N

The mission of the Institute of Management (IM) is to promote the art and science of management.

The Institute embraces all levels of management from student to chief executive and supports its own Foundation which provides a unique portfolio of services for all managers, enabling them to develop skills and achieve management excellence.

For information on the various levels and benefits of membership, please contact:

Department HS
Institute of Management
Cottingham Road
Corby
Northants NN17 1TT
Tel: 01536 204222
Fax: 01536 201651

This series is commissioned by the Institute of Management Foundation.

C O N T E N T S

The recruitment and retention of the right people in the right jobs has always been an important issue for organisations in both the private and public sectors. Now, as success becomes increasingly dependent on the deployment of knowledge and skills, people are the dominant strategic concern.

Most executives and managers recognise the importance of people for their success, but few have a real understanding of what is required to ensure that they have the appropriate individuals. It won't just happen. Successful recruitment needs investment, planned action and continuous management attention.

This book aims to help managers comprehend the steps involved and carry out the effective recruitment and retention of people.

We shall look at one step each day of the week:

Sunday	Understanding the principles
Monday	Knowing where we are going
Tuesday	Getting the best help
Wednesday	What we have to do
Thursday	Ensuring that they are right for us
Friday	Decision and follow through
Saturday	Keeping the right people

Finding the right people

The statement 'Our people are our greatest asset' is now almost *de rigeur* in company annual reports. Yet few organisations continuously plan or act as if they really believed the statement. However, changes have been taking place that elevate the importance of finding and keeping the right people to a matter of *survival*, let alone success. So we start the week by considering and understanding these changes which can be summarised as:

- Advances in technology
- Global competition
- Employee expectations
- Legislation and litigation

Advances in technology

The introduction of the concept of specialisation and the 'Scientific Management' principles of Robert Taylor at the beginning of the century revolutionised manufacturing. It brought mass production and fundamental changes in the management of people. At the time and for most of this century management did not recognise the negative side effects of this new concept. Increasing specialisation drove a wedge between the thinkers and the doers, and – less pertinent to our discussion – it also led to the divisive aspects of the specialist functional fortress.

Since the 1950s, the rapid development of machine tools, computer systems, automation and robotics has been changing the industrial environment. This hard technology has steadily eliminated the unthinking jobs. But the technology has to be managed, operated and maintained by people. No longer are we recruiting unthinking workforces who are expected to hang up their brains with their overcoats. The workforce *now* requires an ever-increasing proportion of skilled workers.

As the management of production processes were wrestling with the advent of hard technology, their colleagues in administration were trying to come to terms with the advance of soft technology. Administrative computing initially moved at a slower pace than automation. Then, advances in hard technology enabled major breakthroughs in soft technology. These developments opened the door for miniaturisation (the personal computer – PC) and user-friendly software (Macintosh and Microsoft). Allied to the converging low-cost telephone technology, these advances have revolutionised administrative, service, professional and public-sector operations. More important from our perspective, they have radically changed the requirements for the recruitment of people. Remember, almost everybody who works in an office must now use a personal computer, but even 20 years ago this was hardly envisaged.

We shall consider these changing requirements in more detail on Monday.

Global competition

International competition has been changing the demands on business. Following the collapse of the Soviet Union, there is now a general acceptance of the market-led economy. The very best recognise this change as a great opportunity. But no organisation can ignore the resulting change in the perceptions of customers. The customer has seen what is provided by the best; and they are beginning to expect it from everybody. This has created a new pressure on staff who traditionally were rarely concerned with customer relations. So, communication skills are now added to the recruitment profile.

Employee expectations

A new attitude towards the employment and development of people is required for tomorrow's business. Management must recognise that the more the demand rises for skilled people, the more these people will in turn want a share in determining or at least influencing their own destinies.

The company that forms a partnership with its people will release massive potential for the good of both the company and its customers. We will develop this theme on Saturday.

Legislation and litigation

This period of change has also had its effect on the relationships between the employer and the employee. While union power has been curbed, that was generally only an intermittent issue for the individual organisation. However, at the same time there has been a considerable rise in legislation which on balance has favoured the employee. Now, a mistake in recruitment cannot be rectified easily by instant dismissal. Termination of employment is constrained by detailed legislation through contracts of service. In addition, the resort to legal assistance in any employer–employee dispute, which was once rare, has now become the norm. Unfair dismissal is an accepted plea for the majority of individual terminations. Organisations are obviously loathe to involve themselves in the cost and possible bad publicity of termination. This adds to the need to take successful recruitment very seriously.

High cost of replacing staff

The process of recruitment or finding the staff we want is becoming more expensive, as we will examine in detail on Tuesday and Wednesday.

There are also other factors, some of which are often ignored. All the elements of change that we have discussed have directly increased the cost of staff. Again, as skill becomes a more determinant aspect of success, so will the lack of the requisite abilities be costly.

The essential point for us to understand, as we continue this week, is that in today's recruitment environment every period of indecision or delay, and most certainly every mistake, carries a substantial cost penalty.

There are some additional issues for us to consider as we plan our approach to the recruitment and retention of people. Some of these concerns arise from the changes we have noted and some are time specific. They can be summarised as follows:

- The Millennium bug and the launch of the Euro
- The shortage of skills
- Educational standards
- Prejudices
- The Internet

The Millennium bug and the launch of the Euro

The immediacy of the year 2000 ('Y2K' for IT specialists) and the launch of the new European currency have brought a problem for recruitment.

The idiocy of accepting the last two digits of the year as a definition of where we are in time for the computer has caused all kinds of problems for business. So many application programs and systems need redevelopment that thousands of companies have a short-term need for information technology (IT) specialists.

In a similar manner, the introduction of the new European currency, the Euro, has created legal and business changes which again mean substantial reprogramming and a demand for specialist staff.

The rigidity of deadlines inherent in the changes and the shortage of IT skills create a short-term problem. But once recruitment has found the staff, we could then be involved in a long-term problem because the need for these specific staff will decrease.

The shortage of skills

All business processes are subject to the laws of supply and demand. That is what a market-led economy means. Recruitment is no exception. Across the whole employment spectrum from workers in manufacturing, through service businesses to public-sector organisations, the demand for knowledge workers has increased much faster than the supply. There is a growing shortage of well-educated, qualified and experienced staff. This is true of professional staff such as doctors, engineers and managers, but it is most serious in the IT fields.

This increases the competition for good people and therefore their cost in terms of salary, bonuses, share options and other elements of candidate expectations. As a result, recruiters are covering fluctuating workloads with temporary or contract staff, 'interim' managers and the use of consultants. They are also paying great attention to the sourcing of skilled people.

An article in the *New York Times* in June 1998 notes that the need for high-tech staff has become so voracious that companies are raiding computer-science departments of universities across the USA with substantial financial temptations. Universities report that there has been a considerable fall in applicants for faculty positions and doctoral programmes. The high demand in this field can cause society to 'eat the seed corn'.

The American Bureau of Labour Statistics provides a sense of scale for the growing gap between supply and demand. It has noted an estimated 933,000 jobs in the computer field, and estimates that this will rise to nearly 2 million by the year 2006. Yet the educational programmes of the USA are only graduating 25,000 students with bachelors degrees in computer science annually. The same statistics are not available for Europe but there is no reason to believe that similar trends are not at work.

Educational standards

Company managers complain endlessly that the educational standards of 'qualified' job seekers have been falling dramatically. Graduates who appear to have little knowledge of grammar, who are unable to spell correctly and who lack basic mathematical skills are held up as an example and feed the scepticism about the educational systems in both Europe and the USA.

However, while the debate rages about what needs to be done to improve standards for the future, business has to cope with today. The wise companies are concentrating on hiring adaptable and willing people and then training them in the further skills they as employers require. We will consider this issue in more depth on Friday.

Prejudices

Employment law provides equality for men and women. On the surface, equality is practised but many highly skilled and capable women have other perceptions. They point to a glass ceiling that prevents them realising their full potential in business organisations. It is perhaps surprising that this should be argued at the same time as the female management style is being extolled as a positive feature for future management. Nevertheless, women advance considerable evidence that their leadership styles are met with scepticism by male colleagues. They receive lower ratings and meet many subtle barriers to promotion from their male counterparts.

But there is another factor in the recruitment arena. Young women are now graduating from universities in Europe and the USA at a higher rate than their male peers. There is also evidence that on average they are achieving higher grades. In this environment, it is clear that the aspirations of women are a key issue in recruitment. Similar prejudices in the development of staff are instanced with regard to ethnic minorities. Another concern is discrimination against older employees – ageism.

The Internet

Earlier today, we discussed the impact of technology on recruitment requirements, but it is also impacting on recruitment methodology. In the USA, the Internet has become a major source of skilled labour. There is now an 'Internet Job Source' magazine designed to cover the growing online recruitment industry.

Employers are investing in national web sites to attract applicants, and job seekers are posting their details on a series of 'Boards' or job centres. In the vast territory of the USA, local Boards were considered a powerful recruitment aid to all sizes of company, but the national Boards can bring more résumés than the employer has time to process. But many recruiters consider the Internet more cost effective than newspaper advertising.

It should now be clear from our discussion that the recruitment of the right people is a crucial issue for every organisation. It is time to turn our attention to two key elements in the recruitment process:

- Who are we looking for?
- What are our recruiting processes?

Today we will consider the principles that lie behind these elements, as a preparation for a detailed definition of what has to be done to be a successful recruiter.

Who are we looking for?

In today's employment environment, it is disappointing how few organisations have a clear definition of what they really need from a recruitment initiative. Executives and management are prone to express their requirements by imprecise phrases such as: 'You know the sort we need' or 'We need good guys: our kind of people'. But inherent in these indecisive phrases are hidden agendas and deep prejudice.

In fairness to many of the corporations who exhibit these tendencies, their motivation is more likely to be based on laziness rather than venality. Their reaction to a request for a clear definition of recruitment policy can be epitomised by 'Yes, we understand that but right now we are far too busy – just find us the right people'. That is not a wicked attitude, but from the viewpoint of the future of these organisations, it is a weak and dangerous attitude.

Our recruiting activities must avoid the hazardous haziness that so often surrounds the definition of need. They start by recognising that many people are going to be involved in the process. They may be within or (as for example in an agency) outside the organisation. It is therefore imperative that we be in a position to communicate a clear idea of what we are looking for to all involved.

Communication
Remember that the purpose of recruitment communication is to help fill a vacancy or create an opportunity and to find a person who is likely to stay with the company. Therefore, there are two elements to our communication:

1 A detailed job description to cover every vacancy, including skill requirements, development expectations, authority levels and interpersonal relationships. Achieving this is a key component of our work on Monday.
2 A clear understanding of the type of person we want to join the family. Will they fit in with us, and do we suit them? Will they share our values?

Value systems

Every organisation has a value system. In the very best companies, it is spelt out, and a substantial educational investment ensures that the values or company culture are inculcated into every employee. That kind of company will take great care at interview stage to clarify those beliefs with the applicant. This is important because the values are not automatically 'soft', such as treating each other with respect, but could include demanding values related to the work ethic or locational mobility.

Those companies that do not spell out their values should nevertheless be aware that they do have a culture. This has been created by the employees acting upon their perceptions about what 'goes around here'. This is not the place to argue the pros and cons of value systems (that subject was well covered by another book in this series *Understanding Total Quality Management*), but there is one aspect which is pertinent to recruiting.

Our recruiting process will evaluate applicants as to how they fit requirements, but we must never forget that the candidates are at the same time evaluating *us* as to how we fit their expectations. For the best candidates, we are probably in competition with other organisations for their services. We should be prepared to answer without waffle the question 'What's different about your company?' A clear value system could provide the best answer.

What are our recruiting processes?

When one considers the growing importance of finding the right people, it is surprising how haphazard is the approach to recruitment in many organisations. Even when clear policies and procedures are defined, the management reaction times at each stage of the process are tardy. Many ideal candidates are lost because of delays in replying to applications, arranging interviews, responding to queries, following up references and finally sending the offer letter. In today's *people market* that is just not good enough.

Management are prepared to accept that the future of their business will be determined by their focus on customers and on the processes that serve customers. These processes are increasingly dependent on people, so management must ensure that a corresponding people-focussed attitude is displayed for recruitment.

Clearly, it is in our best interests to have a defined recruitment policy and procedures in place to facilitate successful recruitment. Most organisations would benefit from a flow analysis of their recruitment processes to see if they operate efficiently and to see if there are opportunities for improvement. Thus, this area will be the major consideration for our discussions on Monday.

Summary

We have spent Sunday emphasising the importance of a successful recruitment system by examining the changes that are taking place in employer–employee relationships. As a result, we have established some clear principles that will underlie our work for the rest of the week. These principles can be summarised as:

- A clear definition of the vacancy; its description, what skills are required and its place in the company
- A clear picture of the kinds of people most likely to succeed in the job and their likely aspirations
- Confidence that our recruitment methods are capable of finding, assessing and selecting the right people
- Assurance that our induction processes and continued development of new people will maximise their potential for the organisation and encourage their personal sense of worth

Right from the start

Today we consider the essential foundations for successful recruitment. Establishing a firm base for the recruitment, induction and development of employees is a key element in the role of executives. It is their responsibility to see that the organisation is properly prepared. This whole area is far too important to be left to chance on the basis that it will be 'all right on the night'.

To ensure that we are prepared to get it right from the start, we will concentrate on the following three aspects:

1 *Policy* – do we have clearly defined recruitment policies?
2 *Processes* – are the procedures and processes to carry out the policies in place and fully understood?
3 *Communication* – are the supporting documents and communication systems available to those who will need them?

Policy

Company policy could be loosely described as 'This is the way we do things around here.' In essence, policies provide the guidelines as to how to carry out objectives. The objectives of recruitment and the management of people which require policy guidelines can be summarised as follows:

• Find the right people, at the appropriate time, to fill defined vacancies

- Make certain that employees are developed to their maximum potential and are used effectively
- Ensure that the methods of assessing performance and rewarding and recognising people are fair and motivating
- Ensure that the organisation operates within the law and within the spirit of the laws related to employer–employee relationships

The development of these policies cannot be delegated to the human resource (HR) or personnel department. Company policies should always be defined by those tasked to lead; in other words, the board of directors. HR should advise, and ensure the involvement of, frontline management.

Before considering these policies in detail, this is an opportune time to develop the relationship between the HR department and line management. This relationship can be the key to success or failure.

The human resource department

In recent years, concern with the people issues in business management has reached significant proportions. The rise in influence of the human resource or personnel departments is indicative of this movement. It is also true, particularly in Europe, that the HR department has grown in status because of increased government employment legislation. Unfortunately, in practice this new focus has been a double-edged sword in many corporations.

On the positive side, the HR specialists are ostensibly interested in people and people management and have some understanding of the behavioural sciences. HR departments generally encourage more emphasis on:

- Education, training and management development
- The motivation and empowerment of people
- Communication and feedback
- Teamwork, quality improvement and similar initiatives

On the negative side, HR departments exhibit all the dangers of specialisation. Once upon a time, the post of personnel director was a general management post, often organised on a rotational basis for key executive development. Today, the lead role is almost always held by a professional HR specialist. Secure in their unrivalled knowledge of the concepts of people management, HR managers win the power to develop and implement personnel policies, procedures and practices for the whole organisation. This can act to the detriment of any innovative culture.

When the HR department has overall responsibility for recruitment, the tendency is for HR to draft the advertisements and kindly 'save management time' by sifting through employment applications to arrive at a final interview short list. They often also sit in on those final interviews; and although, in fairness, they do not usually make the final decision, most of the harassed managers do not really question the initial HR short list. Once the decision is made, HR then issues the hiring letter and organises induction and training. The result in many corporations is that the business steadily becomes populated with 'safe' people who made the short list. In other words, HR decides who is unlikely to give management (or HR) any problems. The new recruits won't challenge the organisation or act as unwanted stimuli with a different perspective. In essence, line management has abdicated its responsibility and fallen at the first hurdle.

Line management
The key processes of business are operated by line management. These people have direct responsibility for

the staffing and management of people in those processes, and they should never allow 'pressure of work' to compromise this responsibility by handing over the task of recruitment to the HR department. However, they would be foolish in the extreme not to involve the 'people specialists' in their recruitment and development activities. Line management should also recognise that the personnel department has company-wide responsibilities of its own. For example, the line manager may view a vacancy as an issue of immediate and *identical* replacement. With a wider perspective, HR, on the other hand, may legitimately question the need for replacement at all, or at least the need for identical requirements.

Relationships

In essence, this issue is a matter of building a relationship between line management and the personnel function. The success of this relationship will depend on mutual comprehension and respect for each other's role. It would be unwise for an organisation to leave the cultivation of this relationship to chance. Executives have the opportunity to foster this mature communication in the process of developing organisation-wide policies for recruitment.

There is no prescriptive or quick-fix set of recruitment policies applicable to every organisation. Policies should be unique to the company and be derived from a combination of their core values and the evolving nature of the business. This does not mean that they should just be allowed to grow; far from it. The development of policies for every aspect of the business, let alone recruiting, should be a continuous process with a strong senior-management focus.

The areas for a clear definition of policy which we should
discuss today are as follows:

- Recruitment plan
- Internal versus external
- Outsourcing
- Induction
- Development
- Classification
- Cost, time and permissions

Recruitment plan

For some organisations, recruitment planning is
fundamentally reactive to events such as employees leaving
or business performance. For others, detailed manpower
planning is central to the management culture. Depending
on circumstances, both approaches are valid and may have
some relationship to the empowerment of line managers in
multi-locational environments.

In the situation where there is no detailed manpower plan,
there is still a need for policy guidelines on recruitment. For
example: is the organisation moving toward a flatter
management structure or looking for opportunities to
outsource functions? This addresses the issue of whether a
vacancy needs to be replaced, as noted earlier.

Internal versus external

The need to develop and retain good employees has
emphasised this area. Policies such as that of specifying
that every vacant post should be advertised internally
before recourse to recruiting externally are now common.
This concept is particularly interesting the higher up the

pyramid vacancies occur. Some companies rarely recruit senior people externally. They believe that their value systems are so vital that they cannot risk leaders who have not been inculcated with these values.

Policy direction is also required in handling recruitment. Some companies manage all the processes of recruitment, including advertising internally, and rarely use outside agencies except for the headhunting of specialist requirements. The more general approach is to use a mixed selection of sources more specifically chosen to meet the need to find the right kinds of employees for different levels or for different environments.

Outsourcing
The move to outsourcing, contract labour and the use of part-time or temporary staff has now become an issue of policy. To a large extent, this movement is driven by the perceived need to reduce fixed operational costs, but there is also an element of providing flexibility.

Part-time and temporary staff have always been an important employment basis for those businesses involved in seasonal or weekly peaks. There is an interesting policy aspect in the growing recognition of the importance of customer care. Part-time and temporary staff are usually omitted from training and development programmes. Yet, by definition, temporary staff are used for peak periods, i.e. when there is the highest level of customer interaction. So in many companies a majority of their customers only meet the least trained and capable staff!

As the pace of technological change increases, there are many new demands on business. Outsourcing can provide flexibility in handling these situations but again poses similar problems to those of part-time and temporary staff. Is there a training or briefing policy for this area?

Induction and development
The introduction of new people into the organisation and their development are vital elements in the motivation of existing employees as a part of the candidates' assessment of the company. They are policy issues, but we will consider them in more detail on Friday and Saturday.

Classification
Employment policy will also be determined by the nature of the organisation. Management principles are similar in concept whatever the business, but the diversity of types of people to be recruited is wide. Just consider for a moment the differing people requirements of the following organisations:

- A mass component manufacturer
- A specialised hi-tech manufacturer

- An insurance company
- A strategy consultancy
- An airline
- A local authority
- A software house
- A massage parlour

Clearly, the differences involved will determine policy and recruitment methods.

Cost, time and permissions
The cost of recruitment and the increasing potential cost of not filling vacancies in a timely fashion are now an area for policy consideration. We will look at these and the whole sector of pay and benefits as we proceed during the week.

At this stage it is important to stress the insidious impact of delays at each stage of the process of recruitment. Good candidates have been lost and weak candidates selected as the result of hesitation or panic decisions in making up for earlier delays. A substantial amount of lag is built into the processes which we will look at later today. But a careful look at the 'permission' stages in recruitment is a fruitful area for policy makers. Many delays are caused by the time taken to seek 'multi-sign-offs' or permission to proceed. A clear definition of needs and policies should allow a greater degree of empowerment and decision-taking at every level.

A continuous focus on the above areas of policy ensures that the organisation keeps in touch with the changing business environment. Another way of looking at the company's policy for recruitment is that this is the first stage of defining the decision criteria during assessment which we consider on Thursday.

Now we must turn our attention to the processes which are in place to support the recruitment policies.

Processes

The process of recruiting involves a series of discrete steps or activities (see the figure). Each step requires an input, which is worked on or processed to produce an output.

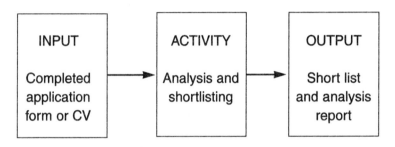

Process steps

This simple diagram appears straightforward except that to function effectively this activity has to meet requirements for the output which in turn determine the requirements for the input. There could be any manner of needs such as legibility and criteria for shortlisting, but probably the completion of time requirements is the most onerous. This problem is highlighted when we realise that this simple step is only one of a series of linked activities which form a process chain crossing departmental and organisational boundaries. In other words, the time requirement on our simple step may be dependent on other time requirements throughout the chain.

The chain or the overall process of recruiting is only as strong as the weakest link in the chain. These linked recruitment activities can be represented by a *process flow chart* – an example of which is shown below.

Planning the process
Everyone can gain from analysing and then improving

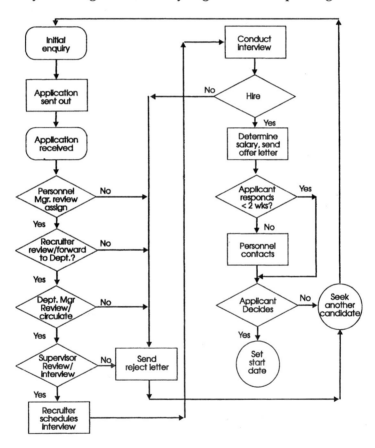

A process flow chart for recruiting a candidate

their recruitment processes. This starts with preparing a similar flow chart to that opposite. Process mapping is a straightforward and simple activity. There are a number of commercial software PC packages available, and the methodology for this is well described in a companion book in this series *Understanding Business Process Re-engineering*. For most companies, the process of mapping will itself highlight potential areas for delay or opportunities for error.

A moment's examination of the chart will show a number of yes/no decision points. Each 'no' decision involves a return loop and a repetition of activities. Other steps in the process will indicate the need for detailed requirements and better communication between those involved. All of these steps produce opportunities for delay and error.

In recruitment, the critical information, communication or decision areas are as follows:

- Sources
- Job descriptions
- Candidate profiles
- Application forms
- Briefings
- A timely reaction

Communication

Recruitment is about people, so the steps in the recruitment process are primarily related to communication between people. Some are direct and written, as for example in documentation such as application forms.

For the process to be effective, each communication step has to be thought about and defined prior to the need. It is too late rushing around establishing facts about a job vacancy or the kind of people we want *after* the vacancy arises. Successful recruiting demands anticipation and preparation. We can start in the right way by looking at the six critical areas noted just above.

Sources

We find our people from a variety of sources. Some are expensive, some are time consuming and others involve a continuous process of seeking a long-term need for specific skills. There are major opportunities to improve our process by avoiding unwise expenditure and the waste of time. We can consider:

- Advertising
- Employment agencies and job centres
- Consultants
- Internal development
- Applicants
- Trawling

With the exception of trawling, each of these areas will be covered in some detail later. Trawling is a planned activity to seek employees on a long-term basis. It can range from regularly presenting the company in a good light to potential candidates, to a focused search for specific skills. Local schools and community activities are the usual source at one end of the age range. Universities and business schools are the source at the other end. Clearly, trawling is proactive and thus the result of policy direction. Therefore, it is likely to be well planned. This activity is not to be confused with the executive search described later.

Job descriptions
The provision of *helpful* job descriptions to aid the recruitment process is vital to successful recruiting. Unfortunately, a high proportion of organisations do not pay sufficient attention to this area. In part, this is because they do not recognise that the typical job description is a structured, formalised document used for internal management purposes. It is not always the best communication document for successful recruiting.

Ideally, for each job there should be a *marketing* description of: the job itself, the range of requirements on the candidate, its relationship to the company structure and peer groups, the pay and benefit range and finally the development potential. Produced in narrative form, such a document would assist internal recruiters, agencies and other external sources and, above all, potential candidates. The production of helpful job descriptions across the organisation requires management involvement and commitment, detailed analysis and establishment of facts, and good communication within the enterprise.

Candidate profiles and application forms
The job description helps to define the skill needs required in the candidate. But recruiters would also appreciate assistance in finding the *type* of person most likely to fit the company culture. This is the purpose of the *candidate profile*.

The application form should be designed to elicit both the formal information required and leads for the interviewing process. The designer should be aware of the key elements in the profile. The principles noted in preparing job descriptions also apply to these documents.

Briefings

Internal and external recruiters together with the
candidates expect information about the company, its
purpose and culture and performance. Specific 'briefing
documents' should be prepared for each, be made readily
available and be regularly updated. These briefings can be
powerful aids to communication and decision-making.

A timely reaction

Finally, the most important area for potential improvement
in recruitment processes. Busy managers are involved in
the candidate interview, review and decision processes.
Their time-management priorities are often determined by
other projects. But if they are not available at the
appropriate time, the recruitment process may falter or fail.
This is another item for executive lead.

Summary

We have spent Monday establishing firm foundations for all the recruiting activities we will describe during the week. We have seen the importance of:

- Clearly defined policies
- Secure and effective procedures and processes
- Clear communication aids at every stage
- Time commitments on the part of decision-makers

In considering our policies and processes, we have realised that we may need outside help, which is the subject of Tuesday.

Selecting an agency

There are valid reasons for using outside recruitment specialists. This is true for both the small company without a personnel manager and the corporation with an experienced HR department. These reasons can be summarised as:

- Specialist experience in a key area
- Economy and time saving
- Overstretched internal resources
- A highly focused approach
- Security, where the company does not wish to reveal its interest through advertising

If we have decided that we do need outside help, there are three aspects which we should concentrate on, viz:

Types of agency

There are a number of categories of specialist and a wide range within each category. There is no necessity to confine our choice to one agency: if we have diverse needs, it may be better to match our requirements through different sources.

The categories of outside specialist help available to us are as follows:

- Headhunters
- Recruitment consultants
- Employment agencies
- Job centres
- Candidate registers

Headhunters

Executive search consultants or headhunters provide recruitment market research and selection skills. They operate in two modes. In one, they react to a detailed candidate profile from a client and search likely companies to identify a short list of possible candidates to fit the need. On the other hand, their continuous research and networking identifies a number of high-quality candidates whom they seek to place with suitable employers.

Headhunters seek candidates who can be identified and have a track record that can be verified. They are primarily employed to search for senior management or people with highly specialised skills. Such candidates are unlikely to answer advertisements and so have to be found and approached directly. The latter is a skill in its own right. A major reason for employing headhunters is that the target candidates are most likely to be found in the ranks of competitors.

Recruitment consultants
These consulting firms can provide a complete professional service which covers all aspects of recruitment. They can advise on job definition, market availability and benefit packages and the most likely candidate profiles. They will draft and place advertisements and assist with or carry out the selection process through to a short list of candidates.

They may appear expensive on the surface but in reality they can save an organisation substantial expense in management time. Although they do vary in quality, the majority provide the security of professionals with wide experience and expertise in the recruitment of the right people.

Recruitment consultants are generally used to find candidates for middle to senior management. The increasing need for 'knowledge workers' has encouraged consultants who specialise in specific areas and in particular who understand the IT market.

Employment agencies
These agencies concentrate on the recruitment mass market for service, secretarial, accounting and computer staff.

Some have become household names with a presence in most high streets. Although often very large national companies, they tend to operate in the local environment to meet local needs.

They will advertise on behalf of clients and provide a limited level of consulting services, but they are primarily used for their effectiveness in providing a fast response in a competitive market. Their high-street visibility and continual local advertising are attractive to job seekers, so they are in the position to bring prospective employees and employers together.

Most employment agencies provide a source for temporary and part-time staff. Some specialise in this area and in the provision of contract rather than permanent staff. This can be a particularly important service for companies who face high seasonality or are project oriented.

Job centres
The Department for Education and Employment job centres in the UK and similar centres in other countries provide a fast and efficient service to both job seekers and employers. They focus on semi-skilled and skilled operatives, though they do also offer a service for professional and executive recruitment. They operate locally but have access to national jobs and applications and are encouraging employment mobility.

Candidate registers
The job centre is in reality a form of candidate register, but most recruitment consultants and now other bodies such as professional institutions maintain a register of candidates seeking employment. Now, as we noted on Sunday, the

Internet is providing a very volatile and popular form of candidate register.

Unlike our last example, most candidate registers are not very volatile. At first it appears very attractive to call for a list of candidates, each with a *curriculum vitae* (CV), at a relatively low cost. But the list will tend to be generalised rather than specific to your needs, and it is quite likely to be out of date so that the most suitable candidates will have already found a job. However, they can be helpful for the organisation that has a constant need for a particular skill or craft, as for example with draughtsmen or catering staff.

Range
Each of the above categories represents a wide spectrum of companies which can range from large multi-purpose international organisations to small specialist units. All have their advantages and disadvantages.

Even more crucial is that the consultants operating in the recruitment market differ widely in their ability and effectiveness as well as their cost. We are seeking to find 'horses for courses', so the selection of the right agency is a vital aspect of successful recruiting.

The selection process

The working relationship between the client and the consultant is crucial to successful recruiting. Remember you are not selecting a mechanistic service but a group of people who are going to work in partnership with you to achieve your objectives.

So the selection process should not be a confrontational exercise which is likely to cause bruises to the detriment of the association. You are trying to find an agency which will reflect your values and standards as well as meeting your technical requirements. At the conclusion of the process, you must have *confidence* in your selection. Otherwise you will be continually checking up on the agency and contributing to an environment of mutual distrust.

Knowing what you want

We saw on Monday that the recruitment of effective people depended upon a clear definition of the job to be filled and a profile of the type of person we wanted. Exactly the same principle applies to selecting your consultant.

The process starts with a clear definition of the assistance we are looking for and the type of consultancy we want. Most organisations have a diversity of need. They can be short term and very specialised or more general and continual. In that situation, there is a temptation to compromise and use the same agency to meet all needs. Loyalty is an engaging value but it is not the answer in this case. There is no need to confine our selection to one agency: we need to find a fit for *each* defined need.

Finding the short list
Previous experience of the company or individuals may provide some names. There are other areas which should be exploited but are often ignored:

- *Executive Grapevine* (a reference book listing all significant recruitment firms and their specialities)
- Networking
- Leavers and joiners
- Reviewing advertisements

Let us look at the last three of these.

Networking
Executives mix with other executives and are generally good networkers. They attend functions, play a lead role in business institutions and mix socially at their own level. Properly briefed by line management or the personnel director on the company needs in the recruitment arena, they will come up with a number of suggestions which they have garnered from their networking.

Leavers and joiners
Many organisations carry out 'termination interviews', but here the tendency is to concentrate on the individual's reasons for leaving the company. A more valuable source of information on how recruitment agencies operate would

obviously come from seeking how the leaver was *recruited* by the new employer.

New entrants provide a similar opportunity to increase knowledge of how recruitment agencies operate as well as providing insights into our own image in the labour market.

Reviewing advertisements
Prospective advisers, by the nature of their business, dominate national, specialised journal and local advertising. Their client's name may feature in the advertisement, but almost certainly their own will be referred to. Analysis of these advertisements will indicate the leading consultancies in each specific field.

Agency presentation
Now that you have arrived at your short list, invite the selected consultancies to present their reasons for believing that they can assist you. Remember the point about confrontation. Rather than putting them under pressure to perform, as conventional wisdom dictates, do everything you can to help them understand what you are looking for and put them at ease. You are looking not for people who can storm barricades but for people who can think and act to your purpose.

Provide each consultant in advance with a clear briefing on the company, its values and assistance needs. Provide a questionnaire and detail the points that you want them to develop. Make clear that you want specific answers to such questions as which individuals you will be working with and the feedback times at each stage of the process.

Indicate that our evaluation will be supplemented by considering the consultant's track record, and that we would appreciate references which will be taken up. Also, invite the consultants to share both their evaluation of our perceived image in the marketplace and any concerns they may have about working with us. Remember that trust is built on honesty and openness from the outset.

However, we should be aware that there are some dangers in making selections and some commonly held myths that could mislead us.

Questions
The purpose of interviewing and presenting is to find answers to a number of questions to help us decide whether the agency is competent and will fit our needs. Some typical questions can be listed:

- What is your business and background?
- How many professional staff do you have?
- What are your areas of specialism and expertise?
- Who are your present and/or past clients?
- What are your methods of working?
- What percentage of your assignments are retained?
- Will you provide us with some references?
- How would you handle a search assignment?
- Who does your research?
- If you carried out a search or selection assignment for us are any source companies or areas 'off-limits' because of other commitments?
- Will you provide a written brief prior to the commencement of each assignment?
- Will you provide a detailed project plan?
- Who will be conducting the assignment?
- What are your fees and charges?
- What is the likely timescale?
- What do you want to know about us?

Dangers and myths

Perhaps the key warning to those involved in selecting consultant companies in any field including recruiting is to make certain that 'what you see is what you get'. Highly experienced and persuasive partners or leading consultants can be very convincing but in practice they may field much less impressive individuals. Insist on meeting the people you will be working with *before* making the decision.

Make absolutely certain that you know exactly what you are paying for from the outset. There is an almost infinite number of ways of charging fees and billing expenses. They will range from payment by results to time expended. Any charging system can be valid unless it leads to misunderstanding and dispute at a later date. Rates also differ substantially but this is not a price-dominated market and so lowest-priced competitors should not be the automatic choice.

Playing safe is not the best basis for decision-making. It's reminiscent of the early days of computer purchase when no-one could be in trouble for selecting IBM irrespective of whether IBM provided the best solution. There is a tendency to select the large multi-purpose well-known company for that same reason. These companies usually are good but there are dangers in knowing whom you will be working with and there could be a lack of focus on your own requirements.

A parallel myth to the last is the idea that all small firms are automatically cowboys. Remember that nearly every large firm was started by an individual dedicated to customer service. The small unit is often specialised and almost always highly focused. Decision processes are direct and short and so they tend to be very flexible and close to the candidate and the specification.

Another myth is that the most well-known or largest agencies naturally attract the best candidates. There is some truth in this, but they also attract a mass audience of applications. The best are quickly gobbled up and there is now an expensive array of chaff to wade through, and possibly they will be presented to prospective clients.

There are some quick-fix solutions that will need careful investigation. Some consultancies will present 'sophisticated' software solutions to candidate analysis and selection, but this can be an over-automated or mechanistic process.

Conclusion
The purpose of agency selection is to find outside help to assist us in achieving our objective of the successful recruitment and retention of the right people. Hopefully, the predominating word that has come from Tuesday is *partnership*. We should now be ready to make it happen, so tomorrow we turn to the methodology of our recruitment process.

Summary

Today we have examined the reasons for using outside help and the wide range of types of agency available to us. We have considered the characteristics of each category and realised that knowing exactly what we want will aid our selection.

In trying to find our specific consultant, we discussed the importance of openness rather than confrontation and noted some hurdles to overcome.

Methodology

Now we must put all our preparation to good purpose. For the next three days we will consider the operational methods that are involved in finding and employing the right people. Today we focus on the methodologies used to find potential candidates. Broadly, these methods break down into three areas:

1 Contingency
2 Advertising and selection
3 Search

Contingency

Successful organisations receive a large number of unsolicited applications for employment. Some will be direct and others from agencies seeking to earn placement fees. These applications can reach 200–300 per week for large companies.

On the other side of the coin, a large number of vacancies are unplanned. General growth will create some opportunities in all functions but the planned recruitment need due to the opening of a new facility or a foray into a new market is the exception rather than the rule. Even the sharp rise in the need for specific skills (e.g. Millennium-bug IT specialists) is usually not anticipated early enough or is just a knee-jerk reaction to outside events.

Too many organisations are in reactive mode to
contingencies, and in the case of recruitment often believe
that they will achieve some balance between unsolicited
applications and unplanned vacancies. Some succeed but
the majority are left with misfits. At the best they are
probably accepting cost penalties from the delay in dealing
with contingencies.

We cannot escape the fact that these contingencies are part
of business life and must be managed. The two key words
are 'Be prepared.' On Monday we paid attention to the
need to define vacancies before they happen and be ready
to explain recruitment needs to those involved. On Tuesday
we looked at selecting an agency so we now have outside
helpers who already know a lot about us and our
requirements. So today let's concentrate on how to handle
unsolicited applications by considering three elements:

1 Response
2 Encouragement
3 Communication

Response
A continuous stream of applications tends to lead to a standard bureaucratic response issued on a tardy basis.

An example illustrates the point. A candidate decided to select a company in the computer industry by sending a fax to each of the most prominent firms. The fax read 'Have qualities you require: suggest you contact me', with an address and telephone number. Of the few who responded, two took about a month to do so. However, the Personnel Director of the 'winner' rang and said 'I have this mad fax in front of me: come in and see me.' The candidate joined that company to the mutual benefit of both parties.

The point of the story is that there are likely to be a few people whom we really want amongst those applicants. Also, we must never forget that the applicants have in many cases decided that we are target employers. An immediate and sometimes imaginative response will help shift the odds in our favour.

Application forms, letters and faxes should never be allowed to gather dust in a pending tray. Every relevant application should get an immediate response, even if it is 'No'. The applicant information should be registered in the recruiting database and communicated to appropriate line management. Clearly, some applications can be rejected quickly but all the others should be treated as if we had specifically advertised for them. In most cases, that will involve an interview. In today's labour market, we cannot ignore potential.

Encouragement
Far from aiming to reduce the number of unsolicited applicants, an organisation should encourage them. The corollary is that they also should be aiming to lift the standard of applicant.

Marketing through advertising and public relations is usually specifically designed to encourage customers. In the new labour market, it would be wise to devote a considerable proportion of these efforts to establishing a powerful employment image.

Every advertisement for a specific post should take the opportunity to enhance the company image. Recruitment agencies, candidate registers and now the Internet should be seen as part of this process. Multi-locations operations should pay particular attention to community projects and creating a warm employment image in their operating locations. Concentrate on creating the view among potential employees of 'I wish I worked there'.

Communication
Effective contingency management is aided by constant two-way communication between operational management and the personnel function. Management must communicate open and timely reviews of pending vacancies and growth plans. Personnel should maintain a computerised database of job descriptions and candidates acceptable to the company. Regular reviews will help

provide information for the later briefing of agencies, the
preparation of advertising and interviews.

The essence of communication is to ensure that surprises
are kept to the minimum, that everyone involved is
prepared and that wasteful delays are eliminated.

Advertising and selection

All advertising is expensive, and recruitment advertising is
no exception. If we are to get value for money, it has to be
used carefully and with forethought. Yet, to look at a large
proportion of recruitment advertising, it would appear that
this expense is little understood by line managers,
personnel departments and even many of their consultants.
Vagueness, unsuitable or misleading words and headings,
irrelevant information and bad layout will attract little
attention and deter the best candidates.

Advertising requires knowledgeable management. If it does not exist internally, then external consultants should be approached. Advertising is a broad term which incorporates a number of types of medium. The initial management aim is to match the vacancy with the most performant type of medium. The chosen medium then has to be used to attract the *right* level and numbers of candidates. The *wrong* kind of advertising copy and layout will attract far too many candidates with a wider spread of skills than we need. This will waste a great deal of time and management effort.

Media

We have noted that the response is the measure of effectiveness in recruitment advertising. If we choose the wrong media, we are lost before we start. However good the copy of our advertising, the acuteness of our interviewing and the attractiveness of our vacancy, they mean nothing if there is no response.

Perhaps it is also worth noting that there are secondary objectives to advertising in addition to candidate response. The company's image helps create an environment which assists recruitment, and some vacancy opportunities can be news in their own right. The public-relations department or consultants should be involved to maximise these secondary objectives. In other words, a news item on BBC radio or TV, both regional and national, is not advertising but will support other media advertising.

The introduction of radio and TV makes clear that the media for recruitment are much wider than national newspapers and specialist journals. Each type we note below can be effective if it matches the type of vacancy.

Whilst other media carry some recruitment advertising, the following are an indicative sample:

National press	*Sunday Times/Times*: managerial/senior skilled
	Daily Telegraph: engineering, sales
	Financial Times: financial, City IT
	Guardian: media, varied
	Daily Mail: middle/junior skilled
	Daily Express: middle/junior skilled
Local press	Middle/junior skilled
Trade journals	Specific skills, e.g. marketing, IT
Radio	Local, skilled
Internet	IT
'High street'	Office (secretarial, admin, temp etc.)
Job centre	Low-skilled, varied

Analysis

Any organisation which is regularly involved in advertising should analyse the effectiveness of its advertising over time in terms of response (number and quality), cost per interviewee and selected candidate and contribution to image. This analysis will provide a good guide to the selection of media and ensure a focus on good copy and layout.

Types of medium
National newspapers

This is clearly the most expensive medium in terms of space, but for management, some forms of clerical work and many specialist areas, it is the most effective. At one time, the *Daily Telegraph* dominated, but steadily the *Sunday Times* and *The Times* have eroded their market shares. The key is that these are the 'sites' that these kind of candidates will turn to if looking for a job, or will usually peruse out of interest.

They provide the advantage of rapid publication, as against, for example, the specialist journal. Their standard of production and presentation is universally high, they are well organised and provide good service, and of course they have wide circulation and even wider readership. These advantages, however, need to be balanced against cost.

Local newspapers
There is a wide range of local and regional newspapers available to recruiters. The great regional dailies such as the *Birmingham Post, Yorkshire Post,* and *Newcastle Journal* and evening daily papers such as the London *Evening Standard* and the *Manchester Evening News* rate with the national dailies in attracting candidates, but of course from a restricted area in each case.

Almost every town in the UK has a weekly 'local' which circulates with variants over all the small towns and villages within its satellite area. The *Croydon Advertiser* and the *Reading Post* groups dominate large populations and the growing vacancy areas of service and 'silicon valleys'. It's worth remembering that these local weeklies pioneered the massive technological changes that have revolutionised the newspaper industry. The best provide national daily quality and service. They are not only powerful sources on the regional level but can also be seen in some recruitment initiatives as an effective support to a national campaign.

Their advantages are that they eliminate the costs of relocation for many posts; they enhance the PR image; and they are less expensive than national papers. Their weakness is that they do restrict the catchment area and are less likely to attract key professionals or senior management.

Freebies

Modern technology has enabled an explosion of 'newspapers' delivered house to house at no charge. These operate with low overheads and rely on advertising for their revenue. Their news content is minimal whereas their advertising content and circulation are very high. In some localities, households can receive as many as four of these free weekly publications.

Their standard of paper, typeface and presentation is generally lower than the established local newspapers, but it is improving and a few are produced to a high standard. In the main, they have been seen as a source of semi-skilled labour only, but that may not be wholly true in the future. They are delivered across the whole social circle or recruitment categories in the most vibrant populations. Close collaboration with the publishers could produce imaginative layout and colour presentations to attract interest in many candidate areas.

Specialist journals

There is a vast array of specialist magazines and journals, of which relatively few are cost effective for recruitment advertising. A large proportion of their readers are impulse rather than regular buyers and in general their purchasing motivation has little to do with job possibilities.

On the other hand, there are a number where the buying motivation is high as regards keeping in touch with employment opportunities. Professional journals such as *The Accountant, Nursing Mirror, Computer Weekly* and *The Builder* are obvious examples. Others, many of them monthly, are advertising outlets which are worth analysis. Their rates are generally low and they are widely read in their respective target areas. However, both varying publication dates and slow response rates are disadvantages here.

Job centres

Job centres, candidate registers and now the Internet all provide opportunities for advertising. They now cover a wide area of vacancies and offer reasonable rates for display with good copy and attention-catching layout.

The Internet has been very successful, even for senior-management appointments, in the USA, and that success will no doubt be repeated in Europe, where the scope will be national. The design of the web sites could be a vital factor here.

Radio and television

Local commercial radio is growing in influence, and the advent of digital television will introduce local commercial TV. National TV is very expensive but does make a massive impact in a short time. Local TV and radio are less expensive but by definition serve a limited audience. All are important to the large company in PR terms.

Posters and classified ads

The familiar boards outside local facilities and sites for the local 'card' advertisements can be powerful for local semi-skilled labour. The rules about effective display that we will consider apply here. Another facet of this type would include 'airship' and 'sky writing' advertising for new 'launch' recruiting.

Presentation

However apposite the selected media, we now need to develop copy and a layout for an advertisement. The objective of the presentation is to 'catch the eye' and then lead the *right* reader to apply for the vacancy.

Catch the eye

The design and placing of the advertisement are key to catching the eye of readers. The design is primarily concerned with the balance between solid and void, the use of headings and small units of copy, and the borders. The style of type, size of the advertisement, use of colour and

prominently placed company logos make all the difference.
This requires knowledge and experience. Some media will
provide assistance in this area, but if it does not exist in the
organisation it can be provided by a recruitment consultant
or advertising agency.

Seeking applications
Well-written advertising with clear information will attract
the right candidate to apply for the vacancy. A lack of
information or vagueness only multiplies the number of
unwanted applications or perhaps even worse reduces the
number of candidates to almost zero. The simple rules to
follow are:

- Clear information about the company and its location:
  detail the product or services and the scale of the
  company together with international links (where
  appropriate);
- Clear data about the vacancy: describe what the job
  involves and its organisational position, some key
  responsibilities and opportunities for development;
- An indication of salary and benefits;
- A precise profile of the candidate desired, including
  years of relevant experience, qualifications and
  skills/knowledge;
- How to apply: detail the name, postal address, fax
  number and (increasingly) e-mail address of the person
  to respond to, data required and the closing date for
  replies (if relevant).

Handling replies

Application letters provide initial insight into the skills and even personalities of candidates. Above all, they highlight areas where information is missing. Some vacancies will need the completion of an application form which must be sent promptly to applicants. In other cases, the CV provided can be the basis for shortlisting or a call for further information. As before, this activity must be planned and ready for implementation.

In some situations, business confidentiality requires that the organisation should not be disclosed at the initial stage. In such cases, the consultant name and logo is used in place of the company identification and the consultant will usually handle the replies.

Search

There are openings where advertising is inappropriate. Senior management or very specialised skills are usually difficult to place by advertisement. The suitable candidates have no intention of seeking another job and are probably happy where they are. Again, where there is a shortage of skills – as for example currently in the IT field – the number of applications arising from an advertisement could be very small. In these circumstances, the candidate has to be 'headhunted'. There are specialised consultants in this area, and to some extent their operations were covered on Tuesday. Their success depends upon their sources and management of information about credible individuals.

We made the plea for close collaboration with selected consultants, but it is absolutely essential in this arena. Clarity in definition of the job requirements and a detailed profile of the ideal candidate will aid the identification of search targets.

We should be aware that the search process can be time consuming and often non-productive.

Summary

We have spent Wednesday reviewing the methods used to attract applications from suitable candidates.

We looked at the:

- Contingent management of vacancies and unsolicited applications
- Importance of timely response and communication amongst all involved
- Role of advertising
- Different types of medium
- Design and copy for advertisements
- Role of search consultants

On Thursday we will discuss how to assess the applications.

Assessment

As a result of the efforts on Wednesday, there are now a substantial number of applications for the vacancy. Our task today is to assess the different candidates to find the right person for us. Assessment is a step-by-step process of whittling down. For our purposes, we will look at assessment as a three-phase process:

- Phase One – establishing the 'long list' for interview
- Phase Two – using interview techniques to find the final candidate or a 'short list'
- Phase Three – verifying our opinions by testing techniques and following up references

Phase One

We noted the need for an initial analysis of the response on Wednesday, but there is a useful aid to note today. Where there is a large response to an advertisement or other activity, it is useful to carry out a crude form of sifting. Using simple categories such as:

- A = candidates who meet all the requirements on paper
- B = candidates lacking one or more major attributes
- C = candidates who fail most of the selection criteria

The recruiter may adopt their own shades of differentiation such as A-, B+ etc. The purpose of this exercise is to reduce to a manageable number those CVs or application forms which need to be examined in more depth to provide the long list for interview.

In the case of technical or highly skilled jobs, it is useful to draw up a preparatory checklist of questions to verify basic requirements. This list could include knowledge of specific software or hardware ingredients or design concepts and project experience related to the job. These checklists are most useful in ranking 'A' candidates.

CV or application form
For more complex and senior applications, the CV together with a covering letter is now the norm, and the experienced recruiter should be able to deduce much more from screening these documents than is actually presented on paper. A word of warning: be careful of natural prejudices in borderline cases. It is better to interview doubtful applicants than to reject them out of hand. Some highly successful appointments have been made in cases where it was not clear that the CV met the initial criteria. Screening 'by the book' would have eliminated these candidates.

For more easily defined jobs and skill requirements, the company 'application form' is a checklist against the criteria required and therefore aids the assessment process.

There is an area worth looking for at this stage, even though it is an interview topic. Has the candidate noted availability time (for example, long-notice contractual terms) or any personal priorities that could influence the selection? These could be cause to eliminate, or be a helpful warning to interviewers.

We must be prepared to handle Phase One with efficiency and in a timely fashion. Wasted time or misleading data collected now could lose a potential winner.

Rejection
We are not in the business of destroying people's confidence or sense of worth. In any case, we may like to consider a rejected candidate for another post at a later date. This is particularly true of senior applicants. When we are rejecting applications at this or any other stage, it is good PR and personnel policy to invite rejected candidates to 'phone' in to discuss the reasons for rejection. For logistical purposes, it is also sensible to provide preferred dates and times for these calls.

Phase Two

This phase is wholly concerned with interviewing, and we will look both at the elements that contribute to a good interview and at the interview process itself:

- Preparation
- Interviewing skills and techniques
- The interview and questions
- Group interviews

Preparation

Once again, the emphasis is on preparation, and nowhere is it more important than in interviewing candidates. Preparation can be divided into two parts: questioning and administrative.

1   Questioning: the interviewer should be fully prepared, which means much more than a quick glance through the candidate's CV. The interviewer should prepare a checklist of the key facts and areas that need to be explored at the interview, which have arisen from a study of the letter and CV. In some cases, this may involve some research into the person's current firm. For example, if the candidate has been, or is, head of a department such as marketing or finance, how well has the company performed in those areas over the last couple of years? Although to some extent dependent on the nature of the job to be filled, many interviewers favour the use of a 'lead form' prepared for this particular vacancy as a helpful collection of notes to aid assessment.

2   Administrative: candidates must be given clear information as to how to get to the interview location, the date and time of the interview, who will be conducting the interview and the likely duration. The room should be comfortable and most certainly not intimidating with the interviewer behind a huge desk and the candidate sunk

into a soft chair. It has also become increasingly common nowadays to record or even video interviews. The equipment needs to be tested and ready before the interview. It hardly needs saying that the candidate's permission must be obtained to record any interview *before* the event. Arrangements to pay travelling expenses and provide helpful information must be in place.

JUST RELAX...
JUST RELAX...

Interviewing skills and techniques
Interviewing is a skilled activity but unfortunately many recruitment interviews are conducted by line management who have had little or no training in the techniques required. It is a senior-management/personnel function responsibility to see that all managers who are going to be involved in this activity are given interview/role-playing training. This is important enough when interviewing school leavers; and it is vital for high-skill or senior-management appointments.

The interview training should recognise the spread of typical candidates, each of whom is likely to be put at ease by different relevant techniques. This short list demonstrates the issue:

- School leavers
- Graduates
- Managers
- Factory operatives
- Clerical staff
- Knowledge workers

The objective of interviewing is to assess whether the candidate matches the company's definition of the vacancy and the desired candidate profile. From that perspective, it should be clear that interviewing is not an interrogation ('Where were you on the night of the 13th ... ') nor any kind of confrontational exercise. On the other hand, it is also not just a pleasant chat to pass the time away. A way to express the two sides of the objective is to restate that we are trying to find the right person and that the selected person will soon be joining us as a working colleague.

Here are some tips for successful interviewing:

- Put the candidate at ease from the outset. Be informal but not overfamiliar. You are more likely to gain the information you need from a relaxed candidate.
- Encourage the candidate to talk along the direction you have planned by asking open-ended questions. Never allow this to degenerate into a rambling monologue.
- Do not ask leading questions where the expected answer is clear. Do not prompt or lead replies but ask

further questions to ensure that you get the candidate's rather than your own answer.

- Stay in control and do not allow the candidate to take over and interview you. Pleasantly explain that you want the candidate to ask whatever questions that occur – later.
- Do not make instant decisions about like or dislike. They could prejudice and influence your questioning.
- Try to develop a continuous flow in the interview rather than a series of 'butterfly' jumps from one subject to another. The planned silent pause may open the floodgates of information, but it needs a skilled interviewer to handle this technique.
- Communication between two individuals involves a lot more than the actual words exchanged. A good interviewer will be aware of body language and other indirect signs of attitude, concerns and personality.
- Take notes but be careful that this activity does not interrupt the flow or embarrass the candidate. The fact that you are going to take notes will be understood by the candidate and so it can be open, but it must not be a diversion. However, where the candidate is giving obviously confidential information, make it conspicuous that you are not recording it.
- Never use your natural power or position of authority to influence your approach. You are there not to impress or put off the candidate but to gather assessment information.
- End the interview with clarity and make sure that the candidate fully understands what happens next. Do not close until the candidate has had the opportunity to pose questions. Answer those questions as directly and openly as possible.

The interview and questions
The interview itself is primarily a question-and-answer session. The nature of the vacancy and the preparation will have determined many of the questions. In his book *The Perfect Interview,* Max Eggert states that interviewers ask only three basic questions – all their questions should fall into these general areas:

1 *Can this person do the job?* Questions in this area are about qualifications, experience and achievements.
2 *Will this person do the job?* Here, the interviewer is questioning attitudes and approach to work.
3 *Will this person fit in?* Does the candidate share the values of the organisation?

Of course, these general questions cover a multitude of detailed questions which are part of the interviewing process. Readers who want to pursue this area further could read Malcolm Peel's book *Readymade Interview Questions* published by Kogan Page in 1988.

Group interviews
The case has been made that one-to-one interviews are false in the sense that the workplace has more generally to do with the interaction between people in groups. This concept has led to the growth of group selection methods and the assessment centre. The success of the military in creating tasks to judge the ability of groups and of the individuals within those groups to demonstrate leadership, innovation and team skills is often quoted to support this approach.

Assessment centres can be a powerful aid, but an over-militaristic approach can be dangerous. In the main, business is not looking for people who are capable of storming beachheads or crossing rivers with two poles and a piece of rope. Intellectual character and strengths have little to do with these assessment methods. There is also the time factor and the need for highly specialised assessors.

More prosaic interviews conducted by a group do have some relevance and can be an element in the assessment process. However, a warning: unless very carefully managed, they can take on the atmosphere of the 'star chamber'. Both authors have been elected councillors in major local authorities. Both squirm as they recollect 'council committees' interviewing applicants for leading officer positions. Highly qualified and experienced individuals were put through the indignity of sitting in the middle of a horseshoe being questioned by people who knew little or nothing about the job definition and had their own political agendas.

Beware of political correctness
Before leaving interviewing, we must draw attention to social issues that interviewers should take into account. In the UK, it is now becoming 'fashionable' for interviewers to avoid any questions that might be evaluated as discriminatory. For example, questions about marital status and the attitudes to spouse, children or other personal circumstances are now taboo. In the USA, such questions can be illegal. However, many interviewers feel that interviews conducted under these rules are not only sterile but can also be positively dangerous. People's lifestyles are a vitally important consideration when filling certain posts. For example:

- Doctors on call could not practically live more than a short distance from their hospital
- Management consultants should not expect to work a normal 9.00-to-5.00 day in their immediate location
- An ambitious 25-year-old may not have the experience or *lifestyle* to manage disparate people in a major project.

Of course, interviewers need to be aware of social and ethnic issues, but that should not put constraints on their ability to assess intelligence, aptitude and personality. People sometimes forget that integrity is a double-edged sword.

Phase Three

Interviewing is the primary selection method but it can be supplemented by a wide range of techniques or tools. These can be used to develop information about the candidate as a type of person. They must be used carefully by trained consultants; a few are of dubious value.

Tests

Today we will confine ourselves to a brief look at the types of testing available. The reader who wants to delve deeper into this area will find Stephanie Jones's book *Psychological Testing for Managers* (published in 1993 by Piatkus, London) an insightful and helpful guide.

The types of test are broadly grouped as:

- Physical
- Aptitude
- Temperament
- Trainability
- Intelligence
- Personality
- Graphology

Physical

Statutory medical examinations in industry were introduced as a means of labour protection in days when children were employed in mines and heavy industry. Today, they are used selectively, more as an aid to suitable job placement. For example, colour blindness would clearly debar candidates from many jobs. In today's environment, the employer also has a duty to protect other employees or the vulnerable, for example patients.

Aptitude

Aptitude is inherent and always present, so aptitude testing is of limited value in posts where achievement is clear from CVs and interviews. However, it can be a very powerful aid in assisting new entrants, apprentices and the growing area of complete retraining. For example, manual dexterity, visual and mathematical aptitudes would play an important part in selecting suitable directions for training, or in matching people to jobs.

Temperament

Tests here may be helpful in examining candidates for vacancies in areas for which they are temperamentally suitable, e.g. sales and presentation.

Trainability

This is a form of aptitude test used in the manufacturing environment, though it does also have relevance in other areas. The test involves giving job applicants a short, highly structured period of training in skills related to the job and then observing candidates carrying out the task for which they have just been trained.

Intelligence

There is a very wide range of intelligence tests. Some can be helpful if used in the context of other tests and interviews, and some are positively dangerous if used as a sole arbiter. The most highly intelligent people can be inarticulate or lack day-to-day judgment. In the vernacular, few jobs require 'rocket scientists'.

Personality

In the business sense, personalities relate to our responses to other people or to situations – in a way the 'half full' or 'half empty' syndrome. So these tests seek to find information as to how a candidate is likely to react to events or view situations. Once again, these tests should be taken together with other evidence, but their results can be very helpful to both recruiter and candidate.

Psychological testing has become a widely used tool in minimising risk in recruiting and career management. It embraces many of the directions noted above. The recruiter is clearly interested in likely candidate behaviour, so it is sensible to turn to the behavioural sciences for help. A lack of knowledge on the part of management has tended to surround psychometric testing with a faint air of 'mumbo-jumbo', but growing experience may dispel that attitude.

Graphology

The analysis of handwriting as a guide to candidate personality is used, but it is a dubious practice. To judge traits such as honesty and propensity to violence from handwriting is dangerous.

References

The final area of verification before making a decision is to follow up references. As the candidates themselves provide these, many doubt their value, but they can offer a different perspective. They should be followed through by use of the telephone which gives the opportunity for perceptive questioning. Qualifications should always be checked when they are critical to the post, as for example in medical applications.

Summary

We have spent Thursday assessing candidates' suitability for filling our vacancy. From the candidates' point of view, it has been a highly competitive exercise as we have interviewed and tested them. Hopefully, we have also learnt how to alleviate some of the stress involved. Now we move on to Friday to make our decision.

The decision

On Thursday we completed the assessment and made the decision. Today we will consider an effective follow-up to ensure that the candidate makes a matching decision and comes aboard as a working colleague. There are three elements to the final decision process as follows:

1 Offer
2 Acceptance
3 Induction

Offer

Making an offer to the selected candidate is not quite as simple as it might first appear. The offer, when accepted, will become part of the contract of employment and will be legally binding on both parties. Also, any oral statements or promises made in the interview or written and implied in the original advertisement are legally binding though usually more difficult to prove.

During the assessment, it is almost certain that discussion will have centred around the nature of the job and the various terms involved. The assessment report should include all these details and possible areas for negotiation at this offer stage.

At the *wage* level, the detailed terms are usually straightforward and specific. They may even have been explained by a simple briefing document. This would include basic rates of pay, overtime rates, piecework rates or performance awards. They will also detail the benefits structure such as holiday, sick-pay entitlements and pensions. In some cases, the disciplinary and termination codes and/or benefits will have been noted. In these situations, the offer letter is relatively easy to prepare and is probably nearly standard. Care should be taken over joining times and dates and reporting procedures.

In *salaried* positions, the situation can be very different. This is particularly true the higher up the scale and if the candidate is approached through search. Again, it is also likely that the possible remuneration packages involve many aspects beyond the basic salary.

The benefits package at senior level can include a variety of items, several of which need to be negotiated. An example of the issues to be considered and prepared for could include any or all of the following:

salary and increments	accommodation
relocation expenses	overseas taxation
annual or overseas leave	arrangements
bonuses	share options
termination notice	probationary period
extra-mural restrictions	healthcare provisions
sickness benefits	pension scheme
expense allowances	family allowances
subsidised meals	sports facilities
provision of a car/car allowance	

Senior candidates, and in particular knowledge specialists, are not only motivated by money or the total remuneration package. We are dealing with expectations related to job satisfaction and a number of 'feel-good factors'. For that type of candidate, these issues are likely to have been touched on during the interview. They may include empowerment and responsibility, and freedom to communicate and to express opinions. Some of these issues will be specific and easy to answer whereas others could be more ephemeral and difficult to answer.

All of these issues must be considered, perhaps negotiated and where possible confirmed in the offer letter. As with the wage employees, the letter should include details on starting and be issued as quickly as possible after the final interview. Delay at this stage can easily turn off a good candidate who in any case may have more than one offer to consider.

Negotiating remuneration
When establishing or negotiating a remuneration package, be very careful that it is generally in line with other terms

within the company. This is particularly important when considering peer positions. Over eagerness to bring aboard a good candidate can bring untold trouble in its wake. Forget any idea that the package is a secret known only to the candidate and a few relevant and trusted employees. The main points will swiftly be known to those to whom it matters. If the benefits are substantially better than the current norm, there will be demotivation, and the new candidate, far from being welcomed, will meet resentment and obstruction.

Once again, the answer is preparation. Ensure that the market rates are thoroughly understood and that internal rates are regularly adjusted in line with the market. Loyalty and commitment should not be seen as to the detriment of the employee.

Acceptance

Hopefully, the acceptance period between the offer and joining is fairly short, but remember there are other factors at work. The candidate may be at the interview stage with competing job opportunities, substantial notice may have to be given to the current employer, and of course that employer may react with counter-offers. All of this takes time, and new concerns may be arising.

The worst policy is to sit there and wait. A concerned candidate may react negatively, and in any case events are out of control of the recruiter. There are three useful rules for this period:

1 Maintain contact
2 Handle new concerns promptly
3 Burnish the 'feel good' factors

Maintain contact

Plan to maintain contact with the *new employee* from a day or two after the offer letter has been sent. Some recruiters opine that if you appear over eager or seem to be pestering, it will have a negative effect or compromise any further negotiations. That is perhaps a reflection on *how* you maintain contact, but the authors have never known candidates put off by over eager employers.

Effective contact and communication is not based on an approach which could be misconstrued as 'Quick, sign up or the job's gone!' Rather, it should carry the message 'Thought you would like to know' or 'Are there any concerns or information we can deal with?' Arrange for the candidate to meet possible peers or attend a helpful company-sponsored event. A prospective employer invited one of the authors to the company's annual dinner dance at a top London hotel. Now this could have been 'sink or swim' but as it turned out, the evening was fun and various personal contacts were identified amongst those present. This produced a warm feeling which was extended on the appointee's joining day.

As much as possible, contact should be direct but in some cases it will be through an agency. Again this emphasises the importance of a partnership with the recruitment agency. Insist that it maintain contact, and recognise that it can be a useful intermediary in handling concerns or eliciting information.

Handle new concerns promptly
Never allow concerns to fester. Always react as if they are genuine (they usually are) rather than new ploys in negotiation. Answer them honestly and seek agreement that the answer eliminates the concern. If this requires a face-to-face meeting with the recruiter or senior management, make certain that this is arranged quickly. Remember that the enemy is time, not the candidate.

Burnish the 'feel good' factors
In the sales arena, this is called 'customer stroking'. Effective interviewing will have identified some factors that clearly made the candidate feel good about the job and/or the company. Note these and seek opportunities to keep them in front of the candidate.

There are certain to be relevant news items or events that relate to the company or the attributes of the job. Short briefings on company success or major achievements in the candidate's discipline can be powerful motivators and create a desire to join the family.

Induction

In the very best companies and public organisations, induction is a key element in employment policy. First impressions are vital and may well dominate attitudes to the company and, as a result, future behaviour. The best value their culture to the extent that they would never introduce a new employee without a planned induction process. Unfortunately, this is not the normal experience of the new entrant.

Pressure of work and a general *laissez faire* attitude create an environment of lack of preparation and 'I don't know.' It starts with the receptionist who has no idea of where to send the eager new employee. 'Perhaps you are on the third floor' is an off-putting reception. Even when the entry details are handled efficiently the driving motivation is 'We need them on the job, now' rather than investing in time for the future.

Pause for a moment and consider *world-class* practice. At Disney sites in the USA, not even a temporary employee would be allowed contact with a customer without a minimum three days' induction.

Induction, therefore, must be carefully planned and carried out. Above all, ensure that it is not diverted or put off because of 'urgent market considerations'. After all, it might have taken a week or two longer to recruit the right person.

The following is suggested as a general guideline to induction, but in many circumstances it will differ:

Before the candidate joins:

- Ensure that the training department is aware of the joining date and any special considerations which should be incorporated into the induction programme
- Attend to reception details – for example car-park attendants, receptionists, switchboard operators and departmental reception – so that these are ready
- Ensure that facilities are prepared, such as office, desk and all equipment needed such as personal computer, office telephone directories and basic procedure books

When the candidate joins:

- Arrange an initial personnel greeting, one organised for collecting necessary documents (e.g. P45) and providing vital personnel information. Issue any documents, security passes, luncheon vouchers etc. that may be needed.
- Make the new employee comfortable with the location. Indicate canteen, parking arrangements, lifts, photocopying or other facilities as applicable.
- Introduce the employee to managers, peers, office etc., and ensure that the employee is secure and will be looked after.
- Ensure that the employee is introduced to or made aware of the organisation's social facilities such as leisure, sport and healthcare.
- Treat the new employee as you wish that you had been treated in the past.

Follow-up

- Within a few days, check with the new entrant's manager that all is okay
- Arrange a semi-formal meeting with the new employee to ascertain a reaction
- Ensure that the induction training is taking place
- Plan formal or informal meetings as appropriate to maintain interest, establish a pattern of regular communication and start to plan the individual's development

We have now completed the essential factors in induction or introducing the new employee into our culture. But if we want our new colleague to stay with us, the process never ends; that is the subject for Saturday.

Summary

Today we have considered four essential issues:

1 The importance of matching the offer with the expectations
2 The breadth of detail to be considered at the offer stage
3 The importance of maintaining contact and dealing with concerns at the acceptance stage
4 The vital part that induction plays in maximising employee potential

Retaining people

If we are unable to retain the people we have recruited, everything we have considered and learnt this week is all to nought. It is also very expensive and self-perpetuating. If people want to stay with us, we are creating an environment that will attract many more candidates. That will ensure that we have access to the very best people and will therefore succeed at our business. Employees *want* to join Marks and Spencer, Arthur Andersen and Sony because they know that they are successful and that in those environments *people matter.*

But the reality for so many is different. Observe middle management at a business conference of a large multi-national watching the video presentation of the company's values. A typical sardonic comment would be 'I wish I worked for that company.' Again, envisage the seasoned employee who joined the firm full of excitement at the new challenge and determined to succeed. What happened to that excitement and spirit of adventure? For too many of our nation's employees, it has been strangled at birth or slowly suffocated by procedures, traditions and downright stupidity. In the full exposure of the global economy, organisations that operate in that manner will go to the wall. But it doesn't have to be like that, and world-class leaders prove it every day.

A whole new attitude to employment and the development of people is required for tomorrow's business. Management must recognise that the more the demand rises for skilled people, the more the people will in turn demand a share in determining or at least influencing their own destiny. The leading companies are already demonstrating that open communication, empowerment and the education and training of their people are decisive factors in their success. The organisation that forms a partnership with its people releases massive potential for the good of both the company and its customers.

There is no prescriptive answer in the shape of a tried and proven set of employment and recruitment policies. But the organisation that wants to improve relations with its people could start by reviewing and assessing every one of its recruitment, payment, communication and development processes, policies and procedures. The assessment criteria should be based on the degree to which each contributes to self-esteem, teamwork, innovation, competence and the desire to drive forward within the values of the organisation.

We cannot cover all aspects of personnel management today, but we will look briefly at the following areas:

- The changing workplace
- Employee focus
- Employee communication strategy – including:
  - culture
  - eliminating conflicting messages
  - management behaviour
- Empowerment
- Teamwork
- Recognition
- Education and training

The changing workplace

The convergence of technologies, the growing proportion of knowledge workers, and the evolution of rising expectations are themselves converging to have a profound effect on the workplace. In particular, the traditional relationship between the employer and the employee is changing dramatically. There is considerable evidence of this change and its likely direction in sections of the service industries and some specialised high-tech areas in manufacturing. However, it takes longer than expected for new patterns of employment to become general. There is still time to think and prepare for this new era in the workplace.

This evolution leads to contracted and subcontracted relationships with employees rather than loyal and committed employees of the corporation. We are already seeing a substantial increase in part-time rather than full-time jobs. Current thinking concentrates on the collapse of trust between employer and employee and the growing lack of security for a workforce. The Jeremiahs are forecasting doom and despondency for the relationship. Yet the reality can be exciting, different and positive.

From the point of view of talented and assiduous workers, this is the opportunity to define and control their destinies in line with their complete life expectations: freedom to choose when they want to work and with whom, and freedom to manage their own time, so taking full account of social interests such as family. The level of wealth for a large number will be determined by their *own decisions* on the balance between work and play.

Employee focus

Employee focus is seen by some companies to be as important as customer focus. Indeed, they see employees as their internal customers who have needs and expectations of their own. They recognise that employees have important knowledge of what is really happening in the organisation. Communication between management and employees can forge a partnership of interest in delighting the external customers. Yet too often today management and employees act as adversaries, with customers the victims of this war. Companies need to establish a communication strategy to be effective.

Employee communication strategy

Developing and implementing an effective strategy for two-way employee communication is dependent on the following elements:

- Creating and maintaining a culture that supports employee communication
- Ensuring line-management comprehension, commitment and skills to support the strategy
- Empowering and involving employees in implementing the strategy

Culture
The culture of an organisation is assessed from the day-to-day actions and behaviours of its members. These are governed by the *real* value systems, which are not necessarily those written down or expressed by its leaders. Organisational culture is established by how management acts rather than by what it says.

A communication strategy should therefore start with some form of assessment of the barriers to communication. In that context, the key points to be covered in the strategy are:

- developing or reinforcing a culture where values come to mean more than words on a mission statement
- communicating company values to support the strategy
- ensuring that the strategy can cope with a vast amount of information and interfaces
- achieving consistency in communication despite different perceptions of language and culture
- using the strategy as a positive agent of change

This all requires the implementation of a communication network which should:

- allow information, questions, comments and opinions to travel through the organisation
- ensure that managers have answers to questions and that they indicate where and how information is available
- build employee trust in the process to encourage feedback
- overcome the barriers to communication associated with different divisions, locations or parts of a unit

Eliminating conflicting messages
Management is prone to sending messages to external audiences, such as shareholders and customers, that are different from those sent to employees. They should ensure that the meanings of these messages cannot be interpreted as in conflict.

Management behaviour

A successful employee communication strategy ultimately depends upon the behaviour of the line managers. Managers who listen to the views and interpretations of those involved are better placed to make decisions. They also help create self-esteem amongst employees because the latter have been recognised and treated with respect.

Empowerment

Empowerment means giving employees the responsibility, authority and resources to act on their own initiative in a growing area of business operations. Empowerment also implies that employees have been given permission to communicate with management about the problems they are encountering.

Teamwork

Teamwork is the basis for a whole new way of working towards delighting customers and gaining competitive advantage. Successful communication of company values is the glue that unites teams in a single purpose.

Recognition

A confident and proud workforce adds colossal value to the overall performance of an organisation. An employee who enjoys confidence and self-esteem as part of a team feels pride in both his or her own work and the success of the company. Management recognition of the worth of employees as individuals is a determining factor in developing this attitude.

Education and training

The most powerful vehicle available to companies to enable them to build a partnership with their people is education and training. Education plays a part in giving employees the confidence to think for themselves within the horizons of the company values. Training is directed towards competence both in an organisation's field and in developing the techniques of management. In this context, managing change is a core competency.

Although executives readily accept the theory of the educational contribution, they rarely put it fully into practice. The education and training budget is usually relatively meagre and is the first to be cut in difficult circumstances. Management and employees need to spend their working lives gaining knowledge; a sensible additional value would be that they also commit to *sharing* knowledge.

Summary

So, successful recruitment also means keeping the right
people. We have noted that preparation and
communication are vital elements in recruiting, and today
we realised that the same elements are present in retaining
people.

Today, we noted that:

- Retaining good people contributes to finding more
  right people
- The workplace is changing
- This change demands a new focus on employees
- Focus requires a communication strategy
- Communication and culture are linked
- Management behaviour means more than words
- Empowerment, teamwork and recognition are
  important elements in retaining people
- Education and training are the key vehicles in
  managing change

Conclusion

This week, we have seen that the successful recruitment
and retention of people requires a great deal more thought
and action than it is commonly given. But we have also
recognised that all the effort is worthwhile.

Further *Successful Business in a Week* **titles from Hodder & Stoughton and the Institute of Management all at £6.99**

All Hodder & Stoughton books are available from your local bookshop or can be ordered direct from the publisher. Just tick the titles you want and fill in the form below. Prices and availability subject to change without notice.

To: Hodder & Stoughton Ltd, Cash Sales Department, Bookpoint, 39 Milton Park, Abingdon, Oxon, OX14 4TD. If you have a credit card you may order by telephone – 01235 400414.

E-mail address: orders@bookpoint.co.uk

Please enclose a cheque or postal order made payable to Bookpoint Ltd to the value of the cover price and allow the following for postage and packaging:

UK & BFPO: £4.30 for one book; £6.30 for two books; £8.30 for three books.

OVERSEAS & EIRE: £4.80 for one book; £7.10 for 2 or 3 books (surface mail).

Name: ....

Address: ....

....

If you would prefer to pay by credit card, please complete:

Please debit my Visa/Mastercard/Diner's Card/American Express (delete as appropriate) card no:

❏❏❏❏❏❏❏❏❏❏❏❏❏❏❏❏

Signature .... Expiry Date ....